Wheels Around Ulster

by

B. C. Boyle

This picture shows the delivery by steamer of Leyland Tiger TS6 (fleet No. 26) to the London, Midland & Scottish Railway (Northern Counties Committee) on 28 April 1934. This was one of eighteen TS6 diesels and an LT5A diesel delivered at this time and was the first 'bulk' delivery of diesel-engined vehicles in Northern Ireland. The LMS (NCC) had taken delivery of two Leyland TS5 Tigers in 1933 and the Belfast Omnibus Company had fitted a diesel engine to an AEC Regal in 1932. These 22 vehicles were the only diesel-engined buses in the 688 taken over by the Northern Ireland Road Transport Board on 1 October 1935. No. 26 became No. 414, and was later renumbered 726 in the NIRTB fleet. It was rebodied in February 1944 and withdrawn in 1950.

The publishers regret that they cannot supply
copies of any pictures featured in this book.

ACKNOWLEDGEMENTS

I should like to thank Mr W. H. Montgomery and Mr R. A. O'Sullivan for permission to use some
of their photographs. Also my niece Honor Craig for translating the script into readable form.

Donegall Place, Belfast. The period would be the mid- to late 1930s as the Riley Kestrel on the left has a CZ registration number (this prefix was only introduced in 1932). Belfast trams were usually known by the name of the manager who was in charge when they were introduced. The two nearest the camera are Moffets, which went into service in 1919/20. This type was later fitted with upholstered seating and more powerful motors.

FOREWORD

I have lived in the Province of Ulster all my life, and have never been far from wheels. When I started school I was taken on the bar of my father's bicycle. Then I got my own bike, and when I started college I had to cycle a daily round trip of twelve miles. During my boyhood I was always wondering what was around the next corner in the road and this led to many miles of cycling through the countryside. The same applied when the car replaced the bicycle. In later years when I worked in transport I served at seventeen different locations so there were plenty more wheels and corners. I never found out what was around the next one!

This photograph of the author was taken on Friday 16 August 1940 at Tyrella beach in Co. Down. That morning myself and a friend, Jack Pentland, who had been at school with me and was then at Queen's University, cycled out of Belfast at 8.55 a.m. on a route taking in Newtownards, Donaghadee, Ballywalter, Ballyhalbert, Portavogie and Portaferry. There was no car ferry to Strangford at this time and we made the crossing from Portaferry on the motor boat *Annie* with the bicycles lashed to the mast. We then continued to Ardglass and Tyrella beach, cycling on the beach even though it was staked and had lots of barbed wire on it to deter invasion forces from landing. We carried on to Clough and Castlewellan and reached Banbridge in the gathering gloom, arriving at Gilford where we both lived at 10.20 p.m. We had been almost twelve hours in the saddle and had covered 103 miles. My bicycle was a Rudge–Whitworth model 5745 with internal expanding brakes, three-speed gear and dynamo lighting. It cost £8 18s 6d and was purchased in Portadown on 4 May 1936. It was stolen from the third floor landing of 10 Royal Avenue, Belfast, on 22 July 1946.

This picture was taken in Belfast on 12 August 1930 following an announcement by the London, Midland & Scottish Railway (Northern Counties Committee) that they had purchased this former linen spinning mill to develop as a bus station (previously there had been a debtors' prison on the site of the mill). Only part of the building was demolished as the new (covered) station was L-shaped, with its exit just to the right of the picture and the entrance in Winetavern Street. Immediately after World War II the remaining part of the mill was demolished in order to enlarge the station. The additional section was not covered but just an open yard. Smithfield bus station was in use for just over 40 years, being taken over from the LMS (NCC) first by the Northern Ireland Road Transport Board, then by the Ulster Transport Authority and finally by Ulsterbus, which continued to use it until 1972. Following the bombing of both the bus station and the neighbouring Smithfield Market in the early 1970s, a new market was built on the site of the bus station. The horse-drawn delivery cart carrying a large barrel was most likely carting goods for Griffith & Co., Wholesale Wine & Spirit Merchants, whose premises can be seen in the picture.

This picture shows the central bus station of the Belfast Omnibus Company in Upper North Street, Belfast, opened in June 1928. Its entrance was in Winetavern Street opposite the entrance to Smithfield bus station, opened in November 1930 and used by buses of the LMS Railway (Northern Counties Committee) and the Great Northern Railway. The open space is still there today and used as a car park. Some of the buildings in the background which front onto Gresham Street have been demolished. Recently some of the buildings in Upper North Street have also been pulled down including the one through which the exit for both the vehicles and pedestrians passed. The Belfast Omnibus Company never bought any Leylands so the two PLSC2 Lions on the left would have been acquired from a constituent company. Both passed to the LMS (NCC) on 26 March 1930 when the BOC routes in Counties Antrim, Londonderry and Tyrone were sold to the railway. The ADC (XI 8746) in the centre also transferred to the LMS (NCC) fleet and was converted into a lorry.

The ELECTRIC Tram is Coming

"Remonstrating" with the Pigs.

Greeting from BELFAST.

A little Entanglement.

This postcard was issued in 1905 to celebrate the coming of electric trams to Belfast – until then trams in the city had been horse-drawn. Prior to 1872 there was a small network of horse-bus services but in that year the Belfast Street Tramways Co. opened the first horse tram route (from Castle Place to Botanic Gardens) and steadily expanded the system, which eventually comprised 104 trams and 920 horses. The Belfast Corporation (Tramways) Act of 1904 allowed the Corporation to compulsorily purchase the company.

Gelston's Corner, Belfast, photographed c.1930 just prior to road widening. The main road, leading away from the camera to the left, is Holywood Road, with the junction of Belmont Road in the foreground and Pims Avenue leading off to the right. Tram service Nos. 27 and 28 ran along Holywood Road to Belmont, and when the trams were replaced by trolleybuses on this route on 26 March 1942 these continued beyond the former tram terminus into the grounds of Stormont parliament buildings. In 1936 the Strand cinema was built by Union Cinemas on the corner of Holywood Road and Pims Avenue. The company was taken over by Associated British Cinemas (ABC) and the cinema is still in use today but now under local ownership. It is one of very few survivors – if not the only one – of the 46 cinemas that were in use in the city during the Second World War and the following decade. **7**

A model T Ford passes a horse and wagon in Donegall Square South in 1926. The bus on the right is an AEC 413 which had been purchased by the then Belfast City Tramways for the service to Cavehill Road. It was put into service on 4 October 1926, making it one of the first buses to be owned by the City Tramways, and was bodied by Short Bros. in Rochester. In 1938 Short Bros. transferred from their base in Kent to Belfast to reduce the risk of bombing during the Second World War, but the Germans still successfully bombarded the factory in its new location. The building on the left (with the wording 'Ireland' on the corner) at the junction with Linenhall Street contained a crown post office and was also home to R. Martin, Son & Co. who were agents for the Eagle Star Insurance Co. in Belfast. Now a listed building, it is currently occupied by a hotel and restaurant; several other buildings on this side of the street have been demolished since this photograph was taken.

Castle Place in Belfast photographed in 1928 when it was known as Castle Junction. At this time a 'war' was being waged between Belfast Corporation Tramways and Motor Department and so-called 'pirate' buses following the discovery of a loophole in the law which meant that the bus operators could compete with the city's trams. The Corporation previously believed that it had exclusive rights of operation in a radius from the city centre up to half a mile beyond the city boundary. Privately-operated buses undercut and chased the city's trams for almost a year until the loophole was closed. The Belfast Street Tramways Co. operated horse trams from 1872, and the trams were electrified in 1905. Under a 1904 Act the Corporation took over the system as Belfast City Tramways (later Belfast Corporation Transport Department) and was in charge until 1973. Recognising their greater flexibility, the Corporation put six buses into service on 4 October 1926 and following settlement of the dispute in 1928 purchased 50 vehicles from the pirate operators. The two buses facing the camera belonged to the Belfast Omnibus Co. which had been set up in 1927 through the amalgamation of 30 small operators. They are both new ADCs – a 416 (foreground) and a 426 model.

This photograph of Portstewart dates from 1926. The track on the street was used by a steam tram which connected the town with the railway station at Cromore two miles away. On 1 January 1927 the trams were replaced by buses. Portstewart's tramway was set up by a private company and began operations in June 1882. Despite never being profitable, it managed to struggle on until June 1887 when it was bought out by the Belfast & Northern Counties Railway which purchased it for £2,100. In 1903 they were bought by the Midland Railway and on the railway grouping of 1923 became part of the LMS Railway. This corner was known as Henry's Corner after S. S. Henry who had a shop here. Mr Henry was also a local bus operator, and one of his charabancs (IW 1379) is in the foreground of the picture. Henry's Corner was well-known as a dangerous bend in the years that the North West 200 motorcycle race passed through the town.

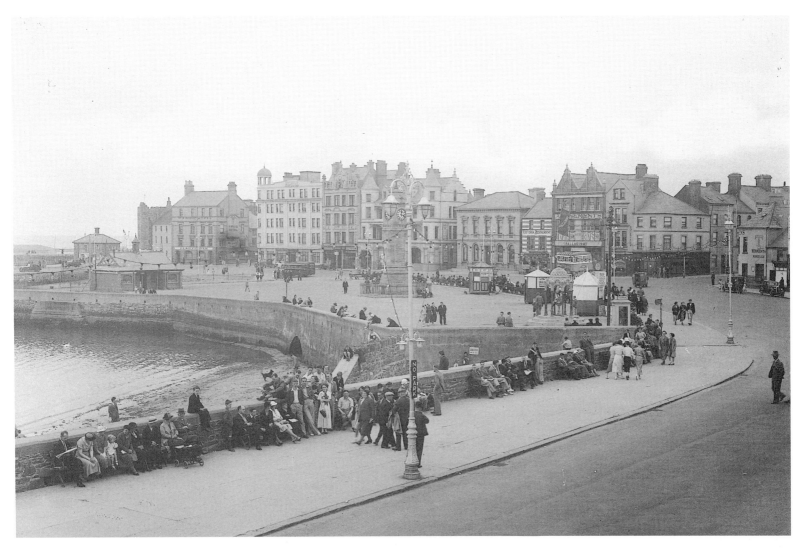

A *c.*1931 view of Bangor, Co. Down, with the principal wheels in view belonging to a Belfast Omnibus Co. bus. The company introduced its first double-deckers in that year and one of these (an AEC Regent) can be seen in the background. Bangor is a well-known seaside resort and dormitory town and at this time was the third biggest population centre in Northern Ireland. The seafront area has subsequently been extensively redeveloped and now includes two marinas.

The buses on the right of this 1935 picture of Bridge Street in Banbridge, Co. Down, belonged to the LMS Railway (Northern Counties Committee) and are seen here operating a hotel tour in conjunction with the Laharna Hotel in Larne, Co. Antrim, which was also owned by the railway. Tours operated in conjunction with hotels were a system peculiar to Northern Ireland and ran from the late 1920s until instability brought them to an end in the early 1970s. Today this wide road is divided into three, with the main thoroughfare (the A1), known as 'The Cut', leading beneath the Downshire Bridge. Two rows of trees separate the main road from the routes to the left and right which provide access to the shops and pass over the bridge rather than under it. Nowadays Banbridge has a bypass which has reduced the volume of traffic passing through the town on the A1.

The Laharna Hotel, originally owned by Henry McNeill, was bought by the Midland Railway in August 1909. McNeill was the originator of the 'hotel tour' concept which was so popular in Northern Ireland. He had other hotels and continued his tours elsewhere after the sale of the Laharna Hotel, whilst the railway introduced its own tours. In 2000 the hotel was demolished and the site is currently vacant.

This photograph of Lisburn, Co. Antrim, was taken c.1929. Today most of this area has been pedestrianised, although traffic still runs along the right-hand side of the road (southbound only) into Market Street and Smithfield Square. The buses belong to the Belfast Omnibus Co., a number of whose founders came from this area. The building with the domed tower is the Market House and Assembly Rooms and houses a linen centre and museum. Behind it can be seen Christchurch Cathedral while in front of the shops is a statue of General John Nicolson who was killed in India in 1857 and is the best known Ulsterman to have served there. The lorry parked at the kerb is a Morris and the one coming down the street is a Karrier. At this time a weekly market was held in the square.

The Pentagon, Ballymena

The Pentagon in Ballymena, Co. Antrim has no connection with the US building in Washington DC, but is just a meeting of five roads. This area has been completely redeveloped and the view as seen in the picture has changed beyond recognition, although the hotel on the right is still standing. The bus is an ADC from the fleet of the Belfast Omnibus Co. As their Co. Antrim services were bought over by the LMS (NCC) in 1930 the scene probably dates from the late 1920s.

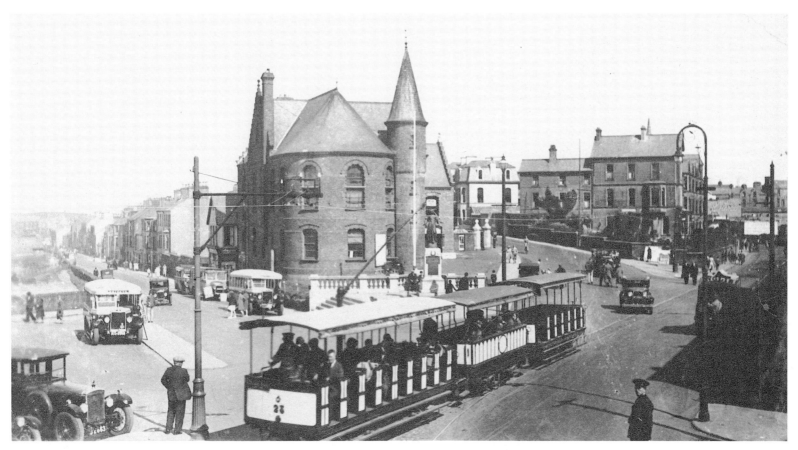

A tram returns from the Giant's Causeway to Portrush in 1933. When it opened in 1883 this was the first hydroelectric tramway in the world, and amazing lack of vision allowed it to be closed in 1949. The system was admittedly somewhat primitive and also used steam engines to back up the hydroelectric system and to operate through the town where the third rail system (with an electrified rail on the street) was too dangerous. *Railway Magazine* of May 1936 wrote: 'The hydroelectric power station [originally] used its 24-foot head of water to drive two Alcott water turbines together capable of developing 104 h.p. These drove a dynamo weighing 35 hundredweight which like the remainder of the electrical system was constructed by Siemens Bros. & Co. The dynamo worked at a speed of about 70 revolutions per minute and generated a maximum pressure (*sic*) of 250 volts with a current of 100 amps. Subsequently more powerful turbines developing 160 h.p. were installed.' The railway was originally intended to run from Portrush to Bushmills and then on to Dervock, but it was realised that it would be more profitable to exploit the tourist traffic to the Giant's Causeway and so the line was continued from Bushmills to the causeway and the extension to Dervock dropped. The buses on the left were owned by the LMS Railway (Northern Counties Committee) while charabancs belonging to Stewart Brothers, a local firm whose main business was a repair garage in the town, can be seen in the background.

From 1928 to 1936 the RAC International Tourist Trophy races were run on a circuit from Dundonald through Newtownards and Comber and back to Dundonald again. This was a very exciting event of the period, drawing large crowds and attracting wide interest. The race temporarily moved from Northern Ireland following an accident in Newtownards on 5 September 1936 in which a car crashed into a group of spectators, killing eight of them. Taken on 29 August 1933, this picture shows the starting point near Dundonald. The race was held annually at the end of August or beginning of September and it was common for bus trips to be arranged to go round the course the week before. The buses in the picture are from the Tonic fleet belonging to J. H. O'Neill of Bangor, Co. Down, and are probably engaged on such tours. This section of road is now dual carriageway and a small monument marks the spot where the race-pits were in those far away days. In 1937 and 1938 the race took place at Donington Park in Great Britain, and although a race was scheduled for 1939 this was cancelled due to the outbreak of war. The TT returned to Northern Ireland in 1950 using a new course at Dundrod, also running in 1951, but was cancelled in 1952 due to the small number of entries. It was held from 1953 to 1956, but following two fatal accidents at the last race road racing in the province involving cars came to an end at that date.

A 30-seater AEC Renown ready to hand over to John McGlade of Armagh on 22 October 1925. He ran a service between that city and Belfast – operating only this single bus – until taken over by the Belfast Omnibus Co. in 1927.

An early AEC bus owned by Smith, McNeilly & Weatherup who operated the Princess service between Belfast and Cushendall via Carrickfergus, Whitehead and Larne from 1924 until they became one of the founder members of the Belfast Omnibus Co. in 1927. Mr McNeilly is the man on the right. Second from the left is David Stockman, who became an inspector for the Northern Ireland Road Transport Board (NIRTB) and Ulster Transport Authority, retiring in 1965. During the 1930s Northern Ireland's privately-owned railway companies found themselves in financial difficulties, and in response to Sir Felix Pole's report of 1935 the publicly-owned NIRTB was set up, the idea being that profits from this would be ploughed into the railways to keep them solvent. The scheme didn't work, and in 1948 railway and road services were united under the umbrella of the Ulster Transport Authority in a new attempt to revive the fortunes of public transport in the province.

This Leyland PLSC2 Lion was one of fourteen buses owned by the Belfast & Co. Down Railway and is seen here at the Square in Kilkeel, Co. Down in 1928. The BCDR's buses were taken over by the NIRTB on 1 October 1935. The railway's main line ran from Belfast to Newcastle and opened on 25 March 1869, closing in 1950. Buses were used to extend the service from Newcastle to Kilkeel; they were originally horse-drawn and operated by Nortons of Kilkeel. On 1 August 1916 the railway introduced its own motorbuses.

The Square in Gilford, Co. Down, 1928. A bus service between Portadown and Banbridge had originally been operated by the Six Counties Motor Co. Ltd. under the name of 'The Pilot'. Six Counties was established by two Scots, Henry Brook of Stranraer and John Hodge of Galashiels, in 1924. In 1927 the company was acquired by the Belfast Omnibus Co., and it is one of their ADC 416s seen here on its way to Banbridge. Known locally as Faith, Hope and Charity, the ornate lamp standard in the Square was erected in memory of Hugh Dunbar McMaster who died in 1908. He was the grandson of the original co-owner of the town's mill. Dunbar McMaster & Co. later became part of the Linen Thread Group. The lamp standard has since been removed, although the rest of the scene has not changed significantly since the photograph was taken.

This photograph shows the bus station on Strand Road in Londonderry at its opening in December 1932. It was owned by the operator H. M. S. Catherwood, one of whose Leyland Tiger buses is on the left. The station was in use for almost 40 years, passing to the control of the NIRTB and later the Ulster Transport Authority. On 7 July 1925 Harold Matthew Stuart Catherwood began to operate a bus service between Maghera, Bellaghy, Portglenone, Randalstown and Antrim and during the next three years built up an extensive network between the towns in Antrim and Derry. In August 1927 he extended his working to what was then called the Irish Free State (now the ROI) when he introduced a service between Belfast and Dublin, and in October 1930 inaugurated a 'minimum fare' (express) service between Dublin and Cork.
His activities in the Free State were compulsorily terminated some three years later by the Dublin parliament which passed an Act whereby the major bus operators were transferred to the railways.
In 1935, under the provision of the Northern Ireland Road and Railways Act his Northern Ireland fleet of 70 buses was transferred to the NIRTB.

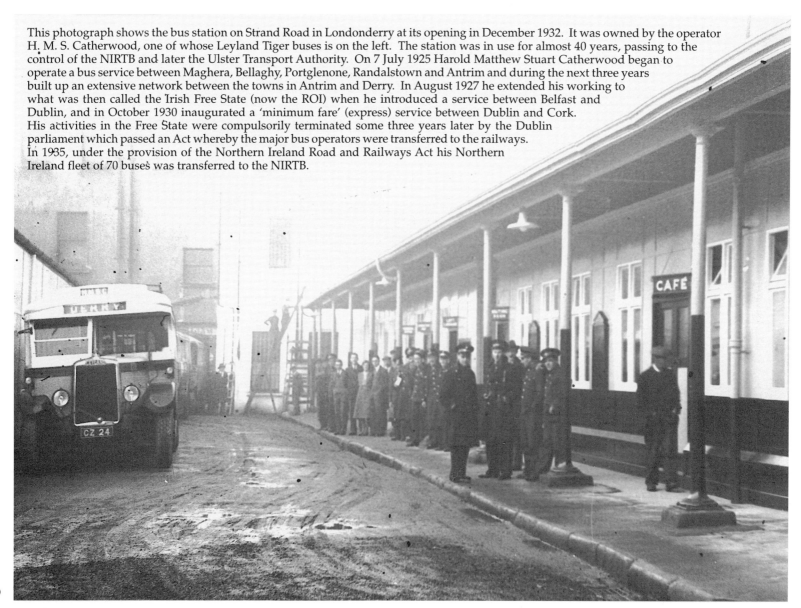

This was one of the last single deck buses purchased by H. M. S. Catherwood before the company was compulsorily taken over by the Northern Ireland Road Transport Board. It is a Leyland Tiger TS6 with bodywork by Northern Counties of Wigan. From left to right the drivers are: Roy Wylie, Billy Cassidy, Tommy McLoughlin, John Glass, Bertie Smyton and John Baird. The photograph was taken at the Custom House in Londonderry in 1934.

The impressive Great Victoria Street terminus of the Great Northern Railway (Ireland), Belfast, photographed on 25 July 1934. The Albion buses outside the station also belonged to the railway, and on this occasion are on hire to Fawcett's of Portrush, one of the operators of the hotel tours which were once an important element of the local tourist scene. On this particular tour the tourists were taken to Dublin by train for the day with a bus connection to and from Belfast and Portrush. Great Victoria Street station was demolished in the late 1960s. The GNR (Ireland) was set up on 1 April 1876 on the amalgamation of four existing railways: the Ulster Railway, the Dublin & Drogheda Railway, the Dublin & Belfast Junction Railway and the Irish North-Western Railway. In 1953 the two governments set up a Great Northern Railway Board to operate the railway, which was in financial difficulties, and in 1958 it was divided between the Ulster Transport Authority and Coras Iompair Éireann (CIE), at which point most of it was closed down.

In the 1930s a service was operated by Belfast Corporation from Hazelwood up the hill to Bellevue using vehicles known as 'toastracks'. This area was and still is owned by the council, and included a zoo, fairground, miniature railway and the Floral Hall (a dance hall at the time, and now used for storing hay for the zoo animals). Like the example seen here, the first toastracks had SD Freighter chassis, but these were later replaced by Dennis three-ton chassis and finally conversions from Leyland TD4 chassis. Operation commenced in 1929, at which point the road had many hairpin bends and the climb for the vehicles was quite steep. The route was subsequently altered to provide less steep and winding access.

A Londonderry & Lough Swilly bus in Belfast on private hire work is seen parked at the junction of Ann Street and Church Lane in 1950. The buildings that formerly stood here had been cleared following wartime air-raids. The bus is a Leyland Tiger PS2 with bodywork by the Ulster Transport Authority, making it similar in appearance to their own vehicles. Established in 1853, the Londonderry & Lough Swilly Railway started out life as a broad gauge (5' 3") railway, converted to narrow gauge (3') and then ended up with no railway lines at all and instead operated only buses. Although the LLSR only owned 14½ miles of railway it was entrusted with the working of 85 other miles which belonged to the Board of Trade in Dublin, which was trying to ensure some sort of transport system to remote rural areas – a very unusual state of affairs and a case of the tail wagging the dog. It began bus operations on 30 November 1929 when it took over four buses from a Mr Barr, expanding its fleet to 50 vehicles including double-deckers.

In 1956 the Londonderry & Lough Swilly Co. bought this Leyland Titan TD4 (R36) from CIE. It had been new in 1937 to the fleet of the Dublin United Transport Co., which was absorbed into CIE in 1945. A Lough Swilly fitter drove the vehicle up to College Square, Belfast where this photograph was taken, and an Ulster Transport driver, Joe McNeilly, took it on to Londonderry. On the left is an Ulster Transport Authority Leyland PS1, while the lorry in the centre is an AEC Mammoth Major belonging to Jos. Rank.

Londonderry is known as the 'Maiden City', and here a maiden from that city watches an Ulster Transport Authority Leyland Tiger PS2 climb steep Shipquay Street. The City of Derry Tramway System, which opened on 1 April 1897, was a modest two-mile, single-track system of nine trams and nineteen horses that ran from Lough Swilly station to Shipquay Place. It ceased operating in 1916, and a replacement bus service (more extensive than the tramway) was not introduced until 1921. Fortunately for the horses the tram routes did not include Shipquay Street. In 1929 H. M. S. Catherwood took over Londonderry's city bus services, running them until they were taken over by the NIRTB on 1 October 1935 and consequently the Ulster Transport Authority and later Ulsterbus.

Co. Donegal had railways from August 1863 to the end of December 1959. The original two private railway companies amalgamated as County Donegal Railways and were acquired on 1 May 1906 by the Midland Railway and Great Northern Railway (Ireland), the latter entering the deal because of its concerns about its rival encroaching on its territory. This connected with the Great Northern Railway (Ireland)'s broad gauge (5' 3") track at Strabane and to do so had to cross the River Foyle. When the Co. Donegal rail service was withdrawn on 31 December 1959 buses took over, and this picture shows a Leyland Tiger OPS2 on hire from the CIE fleet painted in the red and white livery that the company used at the time. It is crossing the bridge which had formerly carried the railway.

McCreary streamlined trams such as this one went into service in 1935/36 and were named after the tramway manager of the period, Colonel Robert McCreary. This one was photographed at the Balmoral terminus on the Lisburn Road near to the King's Hall, probably before World War II. Even if this was a Sunday morning there is a remarkable lack of traffic, bearing in mind that this was one of the busiest roads in the country. On 22 December 1871 J. D. Larsen, who was associated with a company that operated tramways on the continent, attained the necessary powers for the construction of street tramways in Belfast in collaboration with a local man called William Morris. Three short lines were eventually constructed, marking the start of what was to become Belfast's extensive tramway.

Trolleybuses were put on trial in Belfast in March 1938 in preparation for the withdrawal of tram services. Fourteen were ordered initially – two each from seven different manufacturers – AEC, Crossley, Daimler, Guy, Karrier, Leyland and Sunbeam. This is a Sunbeam vehicle with Cowieson of Glasgow bodywork seen in Donegall Square North in 1938 operating the original route (No. 9) from the city centre to Fruithill Park on the Falls Road. Following the success of the trials of the trolleybuses on this route, an order for 114 AECs was placed in June 1939, but when war broke out in September the number was reduced to 87 by the Ministry of Works.

Dundonald terminus during World War II. The route from here to the city centre via Queen's Bridge was converted from tram operation on 16 November 1942, while the alternative route into Belfast (via Albert Bridge) was converted on 8 April 1943. From 1928 to 1936 the RAC International Tourist Trophy motor races were run on a circuit passing through Dundonald, Newtownards and Comber, and this corner formed part of the circuit. It was known as the Dundonald hairpin bend and achieved a certain notoriety. The cars came up the road from Comber on the right and continued towards Newtownards via the road to the left. This is no longer a public transport terminus, although the building in the centre of the picture has survived. It is still a public house, but has been extended substantially to the rear. Traffic lights and new lane markings characterise the roadway now.

An impressive line-up of buses in Queen's Square, Belfast, photographed in 1948 awaiting the arrival of tourists from the cross-channel steamers. From here they would take holidaymakers to hotels as far away as Ballycastle and Portrush. Tourists generally spent a week at these hotels and day tours were included as part of the package. The drivers with the bus nearest the camera are James Henderson and Sandy Robinson. The buses are all Leyland PS1 Tigers built by the NIRTB, whose workshops were in University Street, although these particular vehicles were bodied in a special factory in Dunmurry. The Albert Memorial is in the background; this was built on very soft ground and experienced regular subsidence. It has only recently been properly stabilised.

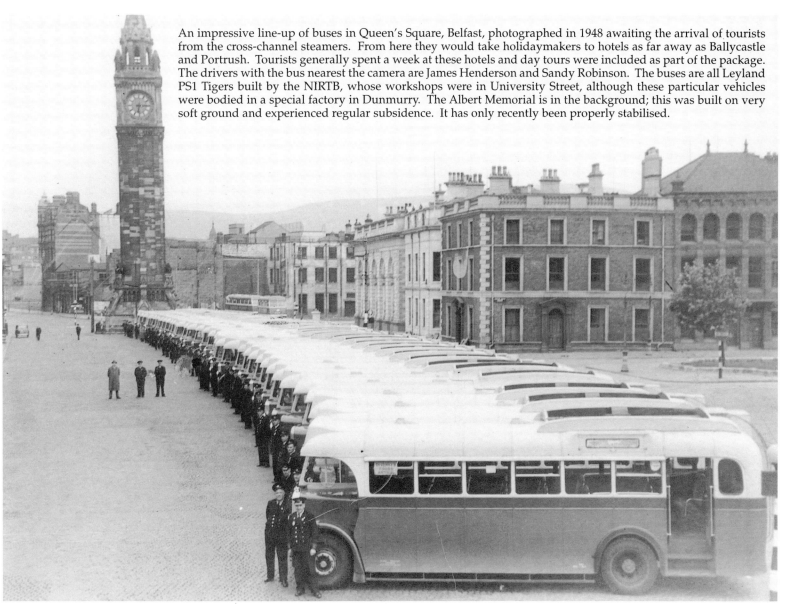

This photograph of Belfast High Street was taken *c.*1953 during the last days of the trams, which ceased to run in February 1954. The tramcar in the centre is a Chamberlain – a type that went into service in 1930 when William Chamberlain (who came from Leeds Corporation) was General Manager and Engineer at Belfast City Tramways. These were the last type of trams to run, operating workers' services from Harland & Wolff's shipyard to the Shankill and Crumlin Roads, terminating at Ardoyne Depot. The trolleybus is a Guy from 1949 on route 31 from the city centre to Cregagh. Trolleybuses were withdrawn in 1968.

Royal Avenue, Belfast in the mid-1950s with the tram tracks still in position. The light coloured building on the left was the Grand Central Hotel, demolished to make way for the Castlecourt shopping centre. The car on the left is a Sunbeam similar to one I was lucky enough to own from 1958 to 1962. Royal Avenue was originally called Hercules Street and is now semi-pedestrianised, with a central lane for buses. The former main post office building, situated beyond the Grand Central Hotel, was demolished at the same time as its neighbour.

Taken from the roof of Belfast City Hall, this photograph shows (in the centre) the former headquarters of the Belfast Water Commissioners, originally a linen warehouse. The building now forms part of a Marks & Spencer's store. The block on the left was the former home of Robinson & Cleaver's department store, but is now occupied by a number of different businesses. Traffic now flows one-way to the right along Donegall Square North so even if trolleybus services were still in operation they would not be able to load where they are seen here. Belfast's City Hall (1906) was built on the site of the White Linen Hall, so-called because bleached linen was sold from there. The City Hall was designed by Sir Brumwell Thomas, and although its exterior of Portland Stone is relatively plain, inside it features ornate Greek and Italian style marble halls and staircases.

A trolleybus for Cregagh loads at Cromac Square when it was still a square and before housing was built on it, reducing it to a road junction. The Cregagh route converted from trams on 13 February 1941. The double-gabled building on the left was a crown post office and has since been demolished. **35**

The Dundalk, Newry & Greenore Railway was owned by the London & North Western Railway, which developed the port of Greenore (including opening a large hotel there) and operated both passenger and freight services from there to Holyhead. The line to Dundalk was constructed in 1873, and that to Newry in 1876. Following the partitioning of the country in 1921, traffic on this line (which included substantial livestock traffic) decreased. In 1923 the DNGR became part of the LMS Railway, but was operated on its new owner's behalf by the Great Northern Railway (Ireland). This picture shows a goods train on 27 May 1939 hauled by a GNR (I) Class A 0-6-0 locomotive (No. 28) leaving Newry for Greenore. Following nationalisation of the railways in Great Britain, this line closed in 1951. The Newry Ship Canal can be seen to the right; Newry was a busy port at this time.

Belfast & Co. Down Railway engine No. 21, a 4-4-2T, has left Knock station (Belfast) in 1935 and is approaching the bridge over the King's Road. This was the BCDR's main line to Newcastle, from which there was a branch to Newtownards and Donaghadee at Comber. The railway also served Downpatrick with a branch to Ardglass. The bridge over the King's Road is still in situ, as is the track bed, and there is currently talk of developing it as a guided bus route. Having opened in May 1850, this part of the line closed in April 1950 just short of its centenary.

Taken on 30 October 1928, this picture shows the new workmen's halt at Frazer Street, Belfast. It was for employees at Harland & Wolff's shipyard who travelled to work on the Belfast & Co. Down Railway. Private cars were relatively few and far between at this time and none were used by the workers in the shipyard. The engine is a 4-4-2T (No. 1) similar to the majority of locos used on the line. One of them has been preserved in the Ulster Folk and Transport Museum.

LMS Railway (Northern Counties Committee) 2-6-0 No. 93 on the new turntable at York Road Station, Belfast, 3 July 1935. The engine had recently been built in Derby and ultimately fifteen identical locos went into service, the later ones being built in Belfast. No. 93 was later named *The Foyle*. The station opened in April 1848 and originally belonged to the Belfast & Northern Counties Railway, being solely used by their trains. Following the birth of Northern Ireland Railways in 1968 a new Belfast Central station was built in 1973 close to the Albert Bridge, and having been made redundant York Road station was demolished (although there is now a station nearby called Yorkgate). The area surrounding the old station has changed beyond recognition since this photograph was taken.

Like the Great Western Railway in England, the Great Northern Railway (Ireland) was an early user of railcars and developed their use extensively over the years. This is the GNR (I)'s original railcar, which was introduced in 1932 with an AEC engine and later fitted with a Gardner engine. It initially had 32 seats but its passenger capacity was later increased to 48. Although the railcar in the picture ran on ordinary bogies, the GNR (I) converted a number of road buses for rail use using a special wheel patented as the Howden–Meredith wheel, which incorporated a tyre inside a flanged wheel for quiet running. With the demise of the GNR (I) in 1958 this railcar passed to the Ulster Transport Authority and finished its days with the gangs lifting the tracks on the GNR (I) line to Londonderry. It is seen here passing through Adelaide station in Belfast, where the GNR (I) engine sheds were also situated. In 1933 there was a rail strike, which accounts for presence of the policemen on the platform.

A scene of two gauges (5' 3" and 3') at Larne Harbour, Co. Antrim, on Wednesday 21 July 1937. Both lines belonged to the LMS Railway (Northern Counties Committee) and the broad gauge line is still in use today. The narrow gauge line opened in 1878 and ran from Larne to Ballymena with a branch to Doagh. It was closed to passenger traffic in 1933 but continued to be used for goods between Larne and Ballyclare paper mill until 1950. The engine is 2-4-4T (No. 110), the only one of this type (S2). The broad gauge line ran from Belfast to Larne Harbour to connect with the cross-channel steamers.

The railway station at Bangor, Co. Down, c.1950. The line from Belfast to Bangor opened on 18 May 1865 and was operated by the Belfast & Co. Down Railway, whose main line was to Newcastle. It remained in the company's ownership until 1948 when the BCDR was absorbed into the Ulster Transport Authority. The buses are Leyland PS1 Tigers, 415 of which were put into service by the NIRTB and UTA between 1946 and 1949. 190 PS2 Tigers – similar but with more powerful engines – entered service in 1949 and 1950. This station has been completely refurbished in recent times and is unrecognisable from this view. The bus station is now situated to the side of the station.

The Royal Ulster Agricultural Show takes place annually at Balmoral showgrounds in Belfast. It is of course a farming event, but before the Second World War and for about fifteen years thereafter motor vehicles were included. This picture was taken at the 1933 show and features the stand of Alister Kirk & Co. Ltd., who where then the Leyland agents in Northern Ireland. A Beaver and a Cub lorry can be seen, along with a KP2 Cub bus. This is painted in the maroon and white livery of the LMS Railway (Northern Counties Committee) and was one of three purchased at this time. It was No. 11 in the fleet, and on 1 October 1935 became No. 384 in the fleet of the NIRTB. The bus was fitted with a twenty-seater body and sold to Harland & Wolff in 1940.

In September 1946 a grand parade of vehicles was organised in Belfast to celebrate the 50th anniversary of the passing of the Act which abolished such restrictions as walking in front of a car with a red flag, and hence allowed motor transport to prosper. This AEC Mammoth had been delivered to Wm. Barbour & Sons Ltd. of Hilden, Co. Antrim (part of the Linen Thread Group) shortly before the parade, and was hence able to take part. It was painted in a medium brown colour.

A second view of the parade that took place in Belfast in September 1946. Visible are a Leyland Octopus (left foreground), followed by a Commer Q4 van, both of which are from the NIRTB fleet. A third vehicle of theirs in the parade was a Foden heavy haulage tractor with a trailer carrying an RAF launch (just visible above the 1911 Daimler on the right). In wartime, launches such as this one sailed on Lough Erne where flying boats on Atlantic patrol were based. The launches had to be taken there by road – a journey of 100 miles.

A Dennis pump escape fire engine belonging to the Belfast Fire Brigade. The engine had a 150 h.p. eight cylinder petrol engine. On board was a 100 gallon water tank, designed to feed twin hose reels. Two hook ladders and a 50-foot wheeled escape were carried. Equipped with a two-way radio, the engine had a crew of six.

The liner *Canberra*, photographed after her launch on St Patrick's Day in 1960 at Harland & Wolff's yard, forms a backdrop to this view of firemen testing the equipment of a 1951 Dennis fire engine from the Belfast Fire Brigade. *Canberra* went into service in June 1961 on the Australian route (Southampton to Sydney), a passage which took three weeks. With the growth in airline traffic, passenger numbers declined and in 1973 she transferred to cruising, carrying on this role very successfully until 1997 (with the exception of a brief period in 1982 during the Falklands war when she served as a troopship). She was sold in 1998 to breakers in Pakistan and was so well-built that they had great difficulty breaking her up.

The short-lived DeLorean Motor Company produced stainless-steel bodied sports cars with distinctive 'gull-wing' doors in Dunmurry between 1981 and 1983. However, DeLorean was not the first car manufacturer in Ulster. The Chambers Motor Co. existed from 1897 and initially made parts, commencing car and van manufacture in 1904 and continuing in this line of business until it ceased trading in 1929. Founded by Robert Martin Chambers (1865–1949) and his brother Charles Edward Chambers (1873–1931), a third brother, John Henry Chambers (1867–1937) worked for the Vauxhall Iron Works Ltd. in London. Along with F. W. Hodges he designed the first Vauxhall in 1902/03 before returning home to join the family firm. The car in the picture is a 1927 model. After closure, Chambers' works in University Street, Belfast were taken over by the Belfast Omnibus Co. as their maintenance works and bodyshop. They continued to be used by the NIRTB and Ulster Transport Authority until new workshops were built at Duncrue Street in 1950.

A Leyland tanker belonging to the Burmah Oil Co. photographed outside their premises at Great Georges Street, Belfast, in 1971. These had formerly been owned by another oil company, Munster Simms & Co. (hence the letters MS on the front of the building). The vehicle had been bought second-hand in Scotland and had originally been fitted with a flat body and owned by vegetable merchants. As a result of this provenance it was familiarly known as the 'fruit and veg' lorry. The area shown has completely disappeared under redevelopment with the construction of the M2 and the Westlink.

This photograph was taken on the A2 approaching Ballycastle, Co. Antrim, on 17 June 1978. The occasion was a rally of preserved buses organised to mark the tenth anniversary of the break-up of the Ulster Transport Authority and the 30th anniversary of its establishment. The leading vehicle is a rebodied Leyland TS6 Tiger which was originally part of the LMS Railway (Northern Counties Committee) fleet. It is followed by two Leyland PS1s of the former NIRTB, which have had to drive over the pavement on the opposite side of the road to pass a herd of sheep, closely watched by the sheepdog.